lithopaedion

poems by

Carrie Nassif

Finishing Line Press
Georgetown, Kentucky

lithopaedion

Copyright © 2023 by Carrie Nassif
ISBN 979-8-88838-154-0 First Edition
All rights reserved under International and Pan-American Copyright Conventions. No part of this book may be reproduced in any manner whatsoever without written permission from the publisher, except in the case of brief quotations embodied in critical articles and reviews.

ACKNOWLEDGMENTS

A Room of Her Own Foundation included "we should have" in their online anthology, *Waves: A Confluence of Women's Voices*, this poem was also featured in a multi-media presentation I was invited to give for their virtual camper series.
Concision published "we thought of ourselves as a lustrous gold" and "this fibrous birdflight."
Coop: A Poetry Cooperative published "we had been born free footed made from frothy cascades."
The Gravity of the Thing published "at this altitude" and "mercury of grieving."
Slow Lightning Press included "let us scribe a plumb line" for their anthology, *Slow Lightning: Impractical Poetry*.
Tupelo Quarterly published "pictures I took from space" which was a semi-finalist in their 2016 Call and Response contest.
University of the Philippines Press published "the fall" their 2017 anthology, *PRESS 100 Love Letters*.

This collection was a finalist in Yes Yes Books' 2020 Vinyl 45 Chapbook Contest.

Publisher: Leah Huete de Maines
Editor: Christen Kincaid
Cover Art: Carrie Nassif
Author Photo: Carrie Nassif
Cover Design: Elizabeth Maines McCleavy

Order online: www.finishinglinepress.com
also available on amazon.com

Author inquiries and mail orders:
Finishing Line Press
PO Box 1626
Georgetown, Kentucky 40324
USA

Table of Contents

in which the floods recede and we can see the foundations of the lost cities 1
lithopaedion 2
nearly asleep in the back seat 3
manifest legacy 4
the unmothering 5
and how when I woke in the morning I knew 6
at this altitude 7
mercury of grieving 8
navigation 9
we should have 10
how many more yesses are in me 11
we had been born free footed made from frothy cascades 12
winter solstice 13
the way my face nowadays slips into my mother's 14
we thought of ourselves as a lustrous gold 15
pictures I took from space
    the midwife 16
    the complex 17
    the hunted becomes the hunter 18
    the fisher 19
    the darkness 20
    the lightning flash 21
    the lost Pleid 22
formerly bisexual woman confronts her newly trans husband 23
the Perseids 24
the fall 25
iterations of a collapse 26
let us scribe a plumb line 27
this fibrous birdflight 28
the night the stars whinnied in recognition 30
notes 31
in gratitude 32

author's note:

A Greek term translated, literally, to "stone baby," a lithopaedion is a very rare phenomenon that occurs when, in a failed ectopic or abdominal pregnancy, the fetus cannot be reabsorbed by the mother's body. Instead, it becomes calcified in order to prevent infection, sepsis, and even death in the mother. I could think of no better metaphor for the sacrifices a parentified child often makes to protect the well-being of its parents.

in which the floods recede and we can see the foundations of the lost cities

when light quivers thinner smells watered-down   is tinny
and the warm stones I cling to no longer hold enough heat

I set down an old trowel and watch your pale eyes squinting
at the sun   in the one cracked photo that remains

I want to chip away at the winces your toddler-self hid
behind a clenched tooth smile and pin curls

to take to steal and hoard them all like overripe plums   to pour
to drink them all in myself then spin the pits over and over with wire

paw at them curious as they dry in the dangling winds
breathe in the tang of your injuries   sharp   like black walnut rind

and hang them to dry along the fallow field rows within us both
sallow mildew-flecked beds of flimsy husks as if something new

could ever grow from the grimy coins you planted
would ever come from the fees you paid   so I wouldn't have to

as if there was nothing left of you   mother
to unbury

lithopaedion

borne of stone mothers
cased within

their abdomens   we
ancient daughters

coil into our own
calcified spleens   this

is how we are safe
from each other

too deep for a blackened needle
to pry ourselves out like a sliver

no glory in becoming such lustrous   such impervious pearls

nor incubating these
milkglass prophecies

of how we might willfully unravel
reduce our selves to gravel to be expelled

like gallstones unmoored from frigid walls
adrift

a diasporum

as if we could make an Eden
from whatever place we claw

to be glacial stone colonists
seeding pieces of us for the others to thaw

nearly asleep in the backseat

when the moon would follow me
gloaming and surreal

tracing narrow country folds

I would be its daughter instead and stalk the leftovers
hunger and hunting

our old territories

what if I swept up the breadcrumbs trailing to your briar patch
strung them like glimmering beads

as if

they were evidence
of how you were broken or why

we were always eating the horizon

manifest legacy

in the beginning here was heat and blood all questions or breastmilk any other was magic we lived to form our mouths into words into tools to fashion names to hold back the ache these pains in our ribs yomping all up in our ears such good students we would string up clear wire and puppet this world with myths to disguise it with Latin terms as though we could fare any better than the creatures we destroy in our crusade to map it all out to plaster these walls with exclamation points

the unmothering

finally shorn of our mahogany hair the years   steamrolled flat
my sister and I untag each other's velvet ears wondering

how it must have felt for you to bleed out
to hear your pulse slow

how your beats
would wane

us small enough to rest in your blonde arms
your   feather breath on ours

seeing you stitch your own lashes back to their raw lids
undoing your old scars   each new welt we wore

how the strong white tendons of your bare hands
first pulled us from your living body

then twisted rubber bands so tight around
we fell away   unnoticed

and how when I woke in the morning I knew

you who had been so content to rest within my ribs
would come convulsing from me on hands and knees

> /how we are all ejected by a centripetal force

> borne of maternal fissions/

to become the first daughter of a first daughter of a first daughter
of the last daughter born two years before her mother died

> /how the egg that created you formed inside of me

> when I was a fetus in my mother's womb/

to be the first child of a first child of a first child
of the last child who was the only boy who survived

> /it was the only winter I was warm   pregnant with

> a furnace   a drummer   an acrobat/

none of us would be here
if it wasn't for a collision vaporizing what we once were

> /leaving ten percent of us rock and liquefying the rest

> to rain hurricanes toward our centers/

a child emerges from the vapor first
and everything else collapses to become its mother

at this altitude

neighing requires the full lung capacity
of that yellow horse bellowing for its mother

      barking across cellophane skies

           slipped loose at the edges

his coughs wrung from the new sun like
pebbles peppering my window

      coaxing me   to the balcony

           air chilled and thick with snow fog

where I finally glimpsed that ticking bird
all week I had heard her clicking

      her siren tapping

           scattering the dead fields

had yearned to see those hidden wings

      so coy

it shattered the dim

      so fleeting

the mercury of grieving

asleep amid salted   among the mire
slunk between the marshes

she is a memory of gleaming
rising from the moss-softened

from her own rotted earth

her dream residue   sticky and
warm tar on sweating timbers

she is a faded underleaf
a curling spiral stranded

her branches sidewindering

and those freight-train questions
she keeps pulling from her knotted hair

all discarded appliances
all landfill rubble

all metal-wobbled thunder

she is and she is and she is
the mercury of grieving

disarming buzzing wires with mittened hands
these ticking   these self-mutilating prophecies

all mosquitos she's still seeking

navigation

sometimes we got each other mixed up the same way I never
felt certain about my rights   or left

your labels were shortcuts
finger spelled into my chest

dotted-lined stretchmarks
scrawled across a map

as if bodies of water
could be held like that

we should have

we house collections of prickled connections
this, the sisterhood of the barbed wire museum

once wound tight over driftwood, wires
long since uncoiled yellow Polaroids ago

these twisted pointed links
thumb and elbow grease crafted

from fence-mending calluses
smoothed away with time

water over rocks
under bridges

we should have lassoed ourselves together
lashed down to weather the storms

built pulleys and lifted our souls
cantilevered the clouds

we can only display these remnants
and inventory our fragments

of ingeniously knotted wires
blackened with age

that we used to raise
to hold back the baked earth

and wax a kind of nostalgic comfort
buffing white-wealed scars from when we got too close

rubbing fractious aches
from standing at such a distance

how many more yesses are in me

I figured that home was almost paid for
assuming we spin a full half circle each day to follow the sun

but since you are the one keeping track   how is it I
am always the one solving for why

should it really all depend on my satisfying you
on these runnings forward as one river which you require

could I not be deciphering the delicate parachutes
of this world instead

would you really grant me this one life
just to watch light stream through your keyhole

we had been born free footed made from frothy cascades

had ourselves borne chains we had never before named
mother or daughter simultaneous particles and waves

suspended lights burnishing in the texture the harmonics

of one dilating chord that approaches   pulses   and   ricochets
splays through and lashes staccato shivers into shade

you may walk as brisk as you like while we haunt this earth
everyone must wait on the tides

clenched teeth foaming at our ankles
burgundy points of sea urchin spine

they tell me perspective is a vanishing line

winter solstice

on the shortest day before the longest night
we wake early on her 21st birthday and drive to the hill west of town

only that was a lie we didn't know when we woke early on
the 21st anniversary of what had been my daughter's birth

of what has now become the birth date of my genderfluid my
firstborn   my spawn

but we would still peer over a flat disk of prairie brushed lavender
by a meek sunrise and drink reddening fields in careful sips

dormant weeds in steaming acres
amber and slippery with melting frost

would sneak pictures of each other from a distance
muffled with scarves behind tiny screens

specks against the white haze of sky
a blank page

spend the sunset at the park by Big Creek
walking to stay warm

where   among the slumbering cottonwoods
I would find more vaginal openings than there really ought to be

open maws in these clusters of soft-wooded matriarchs
and all among those that they had mothered

dark branches veining across the sinking canopy
spilling their night back into the sky

the way my face nowadays slips into my mother's

slatted shadows wedged onto an edge-worn chair

half sunk into the murky corner of a dusky room

strands of shaggy-barked cedar branches look back

reaching for old leaf-strewn and hard-packed paths

that faded turquoise box filled to bursting with only

crumpled newspapers faded and soft with age

the jagged space between two large limbs where they join nearly kissing

trunk split into so deep a hollow as to nearly tear itself apart

we thought of ourselves   as a lustrous gold

a malleable solid   steeped within fleeting veins

that which we sought   that what was got

by this mining   our own pluck   our own grit

we unearthed it with worn shovels   these scars

and stains like badges   like trinkets   like coins

even so   something burrows   a soft

a quieting thing   fettered   and shut   tightly

against its own   twin   self   some part of   us

putty-bare and edible   skinned   and   spiraled

peelings   all pinched   and clamped   shut

against the commotion   this city   of meat

we live in   the ranting the rotting the baggage

within   as if we could   by jaws

by jowl   by cheek   by mouth   if we could

sever   could chew   could only ever   cleave

could hack   could slice   ourselves from it

in increments   or swerves   or in swift in grasping

chops   all this riving   this trying   to split

to pry apart   what   must   only   needs

kindness   to   open

pictures I took from space

the midwife

here is that distant moon here are its scaly scabs it has been battered it has

like all of us
a song

a sonorous wheeze of hisses and harps of lilting pitches
a swooping reach through black space

regenerative and destructive and braking and accelerating all at once
this her

singing chanting lifting opening spreading melding welding melting

and surely it is a living air inhaled and exhaled through her porous stone
her song it has sympathetic strings a vibrating a chorus of young voices

of spiraling swirling exchanges of force as we pass
with overheard words that will never be spoken

the complex

this one is the orange clattering jangle of crowds
heard muffled from the window above
swooping with storming clouds

and then it is the slow sweeping stillness at the end of market
it is the call from a real horn
it bleats like the animal it was sawn from

with its reverberating pulse
its wobbles of indecision this cruxing doubt
it is the humming judgment of all that we resonate of all we attune to

this is all this noise these dopplering distances
they span the icy the existential ruse of isolation
no empty spaces and so many voices within

the hunted becomes the hunter

here is one this is us we are transmitting like a NASCAR race

a roaring a circular a monotonous a powerful

an indecisive toddler with the volume back and forth

the fisher

a static
a humming
a teapot whistle
a slicing
a shopping cart wheel
a buzzing

a gasp

the darkness

here let me point it out to you the tremulous and fading
the what began so shrill this open beak cry calling across

a humid a low sky a
sound-stage-enhanced rainforest

the frog warbling the cicada ratchetting
it is everything vibrating

it is all ricochet over a swampy
over a water rippled soundboard

this bird pleads again this bird pleads again this bird
pleads again for the other to respond

the lightning flash

you cannot see it but this
it is a singular
an ocean wave
a boiling tsunami-maker
cresting and
fractallating

this

this is a lone plane flying overhead
gliding into a deep well
the resounding
the nothing
and into the sea into
itself

the lost Pleiad

but here

this is a piccolo humming
a kazoo made from the susurrating backs of insect wings

a wavering heartbeat

a perpetual boomerang returning and departing
hidden in a seashell wish

a headache throb a message microscoped in tears

the giddy rush of room to grow
from tending inner space

formerly bisexual woman confronts her newly trans husband

I dream I am a wobbly table, but we all know that is really you
whereas I am a malformed gully
you will inevitably tumble into
and blame me for

I dream I am opening a box of flat-pack furniture I never ordered
assembling myself from the scraps without tools
this is
a reoccurring theme

I dream I am sorting through your stacks of refuse
recycling your cants
the sky fills with paper-receipt tumbleweeds
lodged in my fences like matted fur

I dream I am a rowboat made of yardsticks
riveted together from our child's braces
roots bending so we will all appear straightened
unsure of what I am willing to trade for oars

the Perseids

we clambered up the pathway
littered with fractured gem stones

sun nestled into the pillow of her own arms
the promise of a clear night   of meteor showers

dusky winds rasp the serrated trees like nutmeg
across grates carved from cinnamon cliff walls

smearing the clove mud scent of earth
humid and heavy along the bottom of the sky

in the after chill of sunburn   the seersuckered surface of the lake
was a peacock tail   fluttering as it spanned wide the shores

turquoise water sloshed at the edges
sucked in and out through its teeth

he clucked at my stumbling near the cave   he was a magpie
laughing at me   it was the only way we could touch

he was the soft-water lake at Abiquiu
and I drank in the black licorice   of his fever

spinning level with the evergreen shoulders
of Pedernal   grainy in the distance

until the mountain itself strung up a whistling mobile
spider-silk and wire cartwheeling the mulberry ink above

clustered fire seeds dangled so low
we could pluck and eat its grapes

he   a thundering clatter of stone
we   untethered   shooting stars

the fall

screens open
curtains inhaling

                    firefly fingers open
                    inhale me

crisp damp
before the moist leaves

                    leave me
                    wet   turning

have turned

                    me on
          us into

          crickets sawing in pitchy vibratos
          chorusing in rounds

          one takes
          off

          where another one

iterations of a collapse

hustled by tippy ladders
a crocking thud of impact
and silence steaming up
from damp orchard grasses

angels drop from the sky every day
suddenly complicit with gravity
flat-backed and flightless
wrenched fracture of a femur

if even liturgical messengers are tempted to reach
then who are we not to bleed for the fruit?
Eden be damned
the orgasm so worth the childbirth

let us scribe a plumb line

let this be proof that our heads so likely hover

from taut wire weighted by bouldering truth

      right over our feet after all

let our children   fall   where   they   will

and we shall draw them back up each one

      a dipper in a well we can cup our palms around

let us chart the constellations reflected in their inky waters

hew new myths from the thin lines of stars

      already connecting us in this greasy dark

let us migrate these spiraled ladders soldered together

erase and withdraw and re-trace and re-draw

      and finger press the maps into amniotic flesh

let us wend our forked sticks into divining rods

dowse for inner pieces

      dislodge these livers from our throats

let us just begin   to hear it   let us become   ready

to   listen   to how the body   its fibers   their urgings

      how we enact   this   resonance   for how

the violin itself is changed according to how it was played

this fibrous birdflight

this frantic this   hissing   steam
both spire   and   gorge

as though *in*   really could   equal *out*

how we divide   each side
by these two lung sacs

so many sloshing chambers
all twitching flasks

a variegated fetus   and   its
threadbare   its throbbing   tremolos

let every *lub*   be a mitral wing span
every *dub*   a heaving   a feathering   flap

these wavering reds   murmurating cells
swarming   our pouches

the syncopated hiccups of valving claps
so that a small   a speckled thing   expands

contracts
what   else   is   ?

but the daggering
of stretch marks

your blustering intrusions
the steady static of acceptance

of my   yes   yes   yes   yes
yes   yes   yes   yes   yes

fisted hearts straining
clenching wombs   spilling life

cramping tissues in a fibrous birdflight
this enervated meat

we these nubbly   these warblings
all eat and excrete

the night the stars whinnied in recognition

from the concrete stoop of the rented farmhouse
I exhale smoke and cold breath   it floats

dissipating in the star-spattered night   that
pin-prickled Milky Way

all spread-eagled purple and bruised

my accidental offering calls out nine horses
alfalfa-filled hides in scraggly winter coats

shadows of barreling warmth
who invite me to walk among them

nuzzling frosty grass stalks along the darkened lawn

I walk halfway to the road to warn my ride with a torch light
its dangled metal lid clunking like a cow bell

tires churn graveled furrows
whiskering horses part rustling like cornstalks

seeing me off on my way to the ceremony

and when the flaps close on the sweat lodge
steamy earthen magma floods our lungs

sage snaps on scorched river-smoothed stones
becomes ashen nebulae in the tarry heat

reverberations of afterbirth spiraling within us all

notes

"pictures I took from space" was inspired by the sounds recorded in space from NASA satellites. Each section is an allusion to one of the Pleiades, the seven sisters of Greek mythology memorialized in a constellation.

in gratitude

for the many midwives who helped to deliver this stone baby book, including but not limited to:

A Room Of Her Own for awarding me an Orlando Fellowship which was my first introduction to a community of women writers at their retreat at Ghost Ranch. The poem, "we should have" was written there in 2013; "the perseids" was a response to a prompt in 2015 graciously offered by Joy Castro over a picnic table there just hours prior to a hike to Pedernal's collarbones and swim at Lake Abiquiu with the incomparable Bhanu Kapil.

Tupelo Press's "Ten Best" poetry retreat in Truchas, NM, which was a formative experience. Thank you to my group leader, Mark Doty, and to Jeffrey Levine who reviewed this manuscript when it was in its infancy. The poem "at this altitude" was written while there.

Colrain's Poetry Manuscript Conference with Joan Houlihan was key in my ability to conceptualize these unruly gems into the sweet little nest of weirdness that it is today. That single weekend and the people I met there contributed significantly to the development of this manuscript and to my identity as a poet.

Rusty Morrison is one of those people, and her process of reviewing manuscripts to the group, and later, as a personal consultant, was invaluable in providing the objectivity and intentionality that my writing sorely needed. I can only hope I was able to craft half of what she could envision, and will be ever in her debt for her generous feedback.

Haley Lasche is a Colrain alum, and out of our cohort's talk about creating our own journal, she actually had the stones to make it happen. Thank you for creating Concision Poetry Journal, a home for truly luscious experimental poetry, and also, for some strange reason, for allowing my poems to reside in their company.

Erin Elizabeth Smith, Sundress Academy of the Arts, Firefly Farms and the Writer's Coop residency—for accepting me into your rustic cabin in a holler outside of Knoxville, for gourmet foraging wisdom and the biggest welcome a flatlander like me could ever hope to have. The Coop gave me the perfect solitude and nature-immersion to recharge my soul and the devoted time to really get after it. About half of the poetry and all of the final edits for this manuscript were typed by kerosene lamp or scribbled on the porch. Thank you and thank you again.

To Finishing Line Press for taking on this project and creating such a beautiful book.

And always, to M

Carrie Nassif (she/hers) is a queer poet, photographer, parent, psychologist with a private practice, and a creativity coach. Her poetry can be found in the following journals: *The Comstock Review, Concision Poetry Journal, The Gravity of the Thing, Maudlin House, Pomona Valley Review, Tupelo Quarterly, ty(poet)icus, WORDPEACE,* and *Yellow Chair Review*. A new poetry collection, *necessary but sufficient conditions: the vulture girl*, is forthcoming with Saddle Road Press. Recent work can also be found in several anthologies, including. *Slow Lightning: Improbably Poetry* with Slow Lightning Press; *Written Here and There: Community of Writer's Poetry Review 2021, Waves: A Confluence of Women's Voices* with the AROHO Foundation, and in *Cry of the Nightbird: Writers Against Domestic Violence* with WolfSinger Publications (a 2015 finalist in the Next Generation Indie Book Awards, and in the National Indie Excellence Awards in the Women's Issues Category.

Carrie was awarded the Janice Bevilacqua Memorial Scholarship to attend the Community of Writers Poetry Workshop, and the Orlando Fellowship to attend the A Room of Her Own Retreat. She has been a featured writer/artist in the book, *Hearts Compass Tarot* by Tania Pryputniewicz with Two Fine Crows Books. Her poetry has been awarded National Winner and National Finalist for two poems in the Mississippi Valley Poetry Contest 2012. In addition to the workshops listed above, she has also participated in an Elephant Rock Manuscript Clinic, the Colrain Classic Poetry Manuscript Conference, the Tupelo Truchas Poetry Conference, and been a devoted resident of the Sundress Publication's Writer's Coop Residency at Firefly Farms.

www.ingramcontent.com/pod-product-compliance
Lightning Source LLC
Chambersburg PA
CBHW031818110426
42743CB00057B/989